Easy-Step B

Houseplants

Contents

Introduction

An indoor garden is a source of pleasure and interest to all those who see it. Houseplants add a lovely and decorative element to a home as they grow and blossom. People around the world have been cultivating plants indoors for thousands of years. In fact, houseplants are domesticated wild plants that have, over many years, been bred to grow indoors. They can withstand and even thrive in the home environment, where sunlight is limited or filtered, temperatures vary widely, and humidity is low.

The next time you see a houseplant that you like, buy it and bring it home. This book will help you learn to take care of it. You will find information on selecting and preparing the right-sized pot for a new plant, as well as how to plant it correctly. This book explains the varying light needs of houseplants and how to situate them accordingly. Over time, plants require watering, fertilizing, and possibly pruning. This book shows you how to do all of these things so your plants will continue to thrive. Should problems arise, either with growing conditions or from pests or disease, you can identify the culprit and take measures to correct the situation. Finally, a section on propagation is included. Many home gardeners find it easy and satisfying to create new plants from old ones—this book shows you how.

Selecting Houseplants

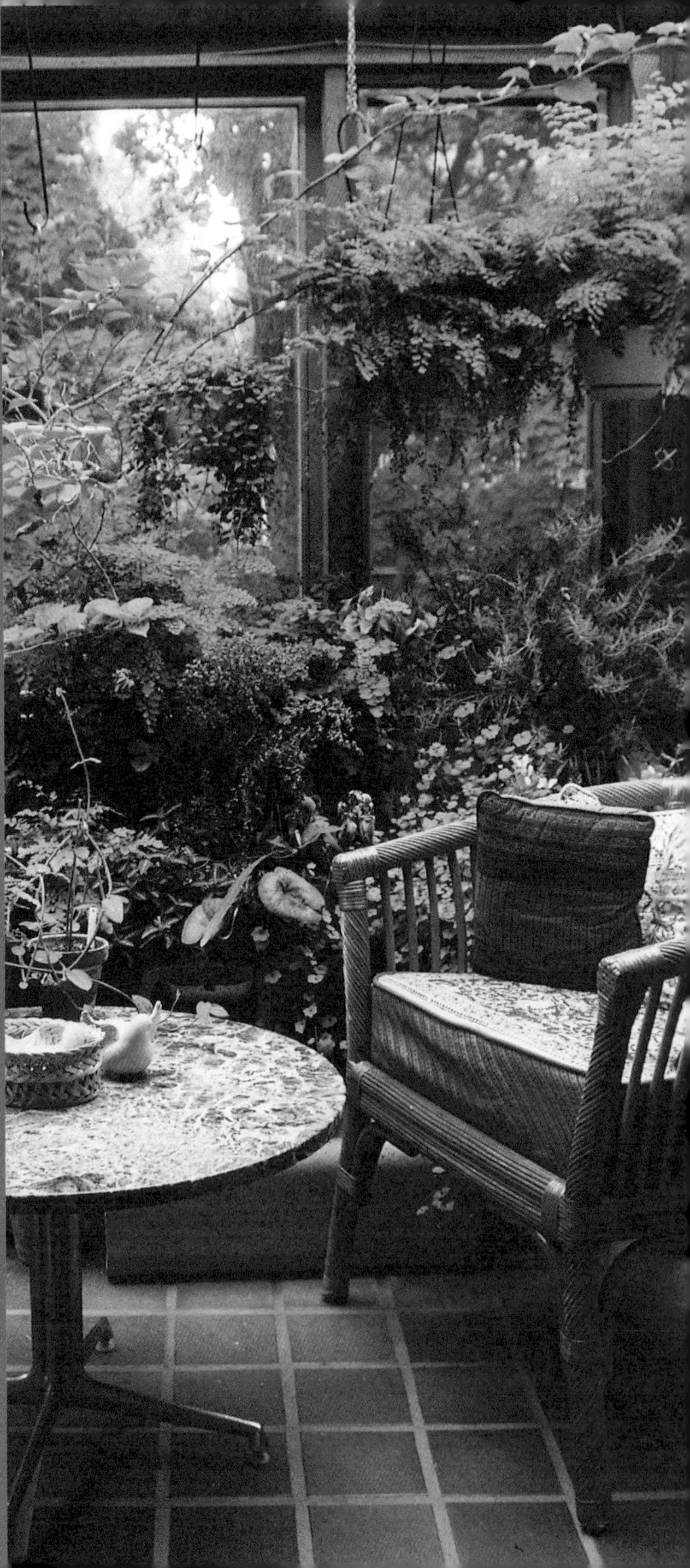

1

Enhance your home

Attractive foliage and flowering plants make useful, relatively inexpensive interior design elements. Plants add life and warmth to homes. They can fill a variety of needs and be an important part of the decorative scheme of the room. Plants can add color, alter the scale, fill empty spaces, help create divisions within a room, and obscure architectural defects. Each room has a certain size, mood, function, and color scheme, and plants can be used to enhance each one's particular atmosphere.

2 Choose plant locations

When arranging, grouping, and positioning plants, consider not only the appearance of the plant itself, but also the container it is in and the background against which it will be seen. Also consider the features or furniture that surround it, and its compatibility with the microclimate in which it will live. Verify that the plant will have enough space to grow and the appropriate amount of light. Finally, make sure that it will serve the need you have for it in your home.

3

Decide where to shop

Garden centers, florists, and interior plant stores are usually the best places to look for house-plants. Choose reputable stores where the plants receive proper care. Buying plants at the super-market or from a truck parked at a gas station may be risky. Plants sold this way have most likely not be acclimatized, and their growing and shipping conditions may have been far from ideal. Some houseplant varieties may be available only by mail (be sure the company has a money-back guar-antee) or from a plant society.

4 Choose the right types

Ask yourself a few questions when choosing houseplants: What kind of plants do you like? Flowering plants? Foliage plants? Cacti? Do you prefer plants that are upright or hanging? Ones with small or large leaves? Consider also the size (now and at maturity), shape, and texture of the plant—tall and arching, low and bushy, soft and feathery, as well as columnar, strong, and graphical.

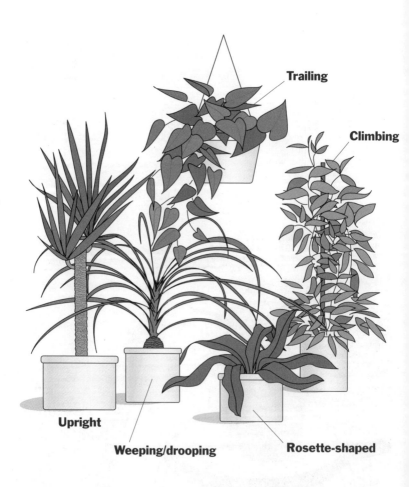

Trailing

Climbing

Upright

Weeping/drooping

Rosette-shaped

When you go to buy a new plant, know where in your house you'd like to put it so you can choose a plant of the right size. Note the lighting, temperature, and humidity of the location and buy a plant that is well suited to that environment. Consider also the amount of care you are able to give the plant. If you don't have a lot of time to spend tending plants, buy mature ones that can adapt to many kinds of lighting, humidity, watering, and temperature conditions.

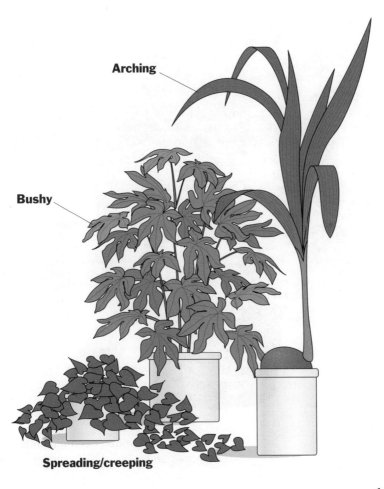

Arching

Bushy

Spreading/creeping

SELECTING HOUSEPLANTS

5 Buy healthy plants

Select a plant with a nice overall shape, and check
it carefully for any signs of damage. Inspect leaves
and stems for pests or diseases. Look at the color
of the leaves and whether the plant shows signs
of new growth. Check for brown edges on leaves or any
evidence that damaged leaf areas may have been cut away.
Leaves should be free from dust and grime, but should not
look unnaturally shiny. Check the soil with your fingers.
It shouldn't be too loose or too compact.

Look for . . .

Strong stems

Healthy topgrowth

Leaves of
good color

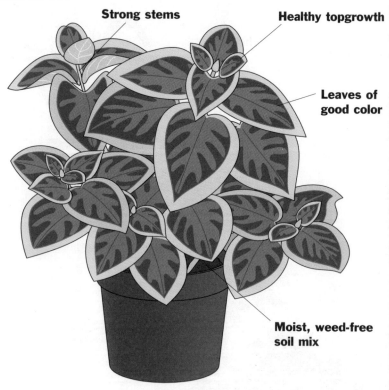

Moist, weed-free
soil mix

TIP: New plants often need repotting.
See pages 18 to 25.

Check for roots growing out of the bottom of the pot or above the surface of the soil. These indicate that the plant has outgrown its container and needs to be repotted in a larger one. Choose flowering plants with lots of buds rather than ones in full bloom so you can enjoy the flowers longer. Prepare plants for the ride home. Warm the car in winter and make sure plants are wrapped. In the summer, buy ones with well-moistened soil. If it is windy, wrap the plants in heavy plastic or cloth until you get them home.

Avoid plants with . . .

Thin topgrowth

Brown edges

Pale leaves

Dried-out soil mix

Provide enough light

In general, foliage plants need less light than flowering plants, and plants with variegated leaves (ones with areas of white, yellow, or other colors mixed in with the green) need more light than all-green varieties. Most houseplants prefer plenty of partial sun or indirect light rather than direct sunlight. When studying the lighting conditions in your home, consider both the intensity of the light and its duration (the length of time the light hits that particular spot). Choose plants accordingly.

High light/full sun

Found in a greenhouse or by a window with a southern or southwestern exposure. This is intense light—as strong as can be found indoors.

Medium light/filtered sun

Refers to direct exposure from an east or west window, or near a filtered southern or southwestern exposure, or some distance from a southern or southwestern exposure that is unfiltered.

Low light/light shade

Found near north-facing windows, or several feet from an east or west window, or far from a southern or southwestern exposure. It is common in corners and bathrooms.

Too much light will cause a plant to wilt and its leaves to fade. Too little light forces a plant to drop its leaves and to grow ones that are unusually thin and long. Increase the light available by using a fluorescent light fixture, preferably with one "cool white" and one "warm white" bulb. Incandescent bulbs (the usual light bulbs) won't help. They put out more heat than light—if a plant is close enough to one to get enough light, it will burn.

Sunny (curtains open)   **Filtered sun (sheer curtain)**

T I P : Plants often grow toward the strongest light source. Rotate plants for a balanced shape.

Light shade

Planting for Best Growth

1

Let plants adjust

Houseplants need to adjust to new surroundings and may go through a mild case of shock when first brought home. The adjustment may take several weeks. At first, leaves may yellow and blossoms may drop. A plant that normally tolerates low light was probably grown under strong light. Place it in two interim locations with decreasing light intensity (a month in each) before placing it in its final spot. Once a plant is used to its permanent location, keep the surrounding environmental factors consistent.

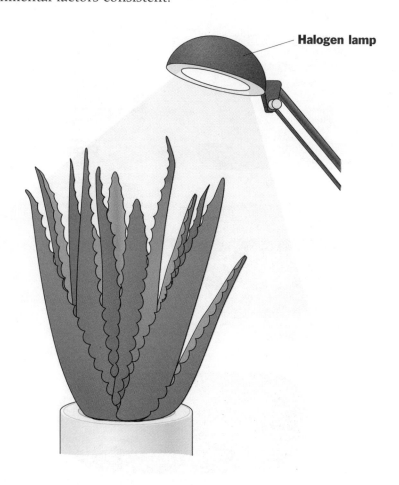

Halogen lamp

2 Select containers

The container it is planted in directly influences a plant's growth and appearance—and what kind of care it will need. All planting pots must have drainage holes. Clay and plastic pots are available in many shapes and sizes, generally ranging from 2 to 18 inches in diameter. Plastic pots are lighter, less expensive, and retain water better than clay ones but require potting mixes with excellent drainage. Soak new clay pots in water for several hours before planting, or the clay will absorb water from the potting soil, drying it out.

Clay

Ceramic

Ceramic

Plastic

Clay

Use plastic or glazed ceramic saucers under pots. Add a round of ½-inch-thick cork under clay saucers. Scrub previously used pots with warm water and a stiff brush, or soak them in a 1:10 solution of laundry bleach and water, then rinse with clear water. Both plastic and clay pots can be placed inside a decorative container—a cachepot or jardiniere. Baskets with a plastic saucer inside can also be used. Make sure the decorative outer container is at least 2 inches higher than the pot the plant is growing in.

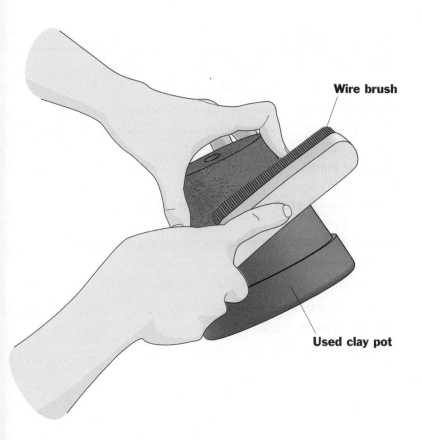

Wire brush

Used clay pot

Use good potting mix

Unless you have a place to prepare potting mixes, time to do the work, and a source of ingredients, it is easier to buy ready-to-use mixes. There are many brands available, and some are better than others. Ask for recommendations from the staff at a local nursery or plant store. Make sure the mix is appropriate for your plant and that it's light enough to provide drainage and air movement in the root zone. If the prepackaged mixes do not drain well, you can lighten them with perlite, pumice, or vermiculite.

Useful Additives

Aggregate   Made of clay pellets. Provides drainage.

Bark chips   Hold water and added fertilizer.

Charcoal   Absorbs excess minerals and waste.

Coarse sand   Loosens up potting mixtures, providing better aeration and drainage.

Dolomite limestone powder   Helps reduce the acidity of potting mixtures.

Eggshell/oyster shell   Reduces the acidity and assists drainage of potting mixtures.

Humus (leaf mold)   Retains nutrients and gives an open texture.

Limestone chips   Reduces the acidity and assists drainage.

Peat moss   Holds water and added fertilizer.

Perlite   Increases aeration and drainage.

Sphagnum moss   Helps retain water.

Vermiculite   Absorbs and retains nutrients and water.

Prepare homemade mixes

If you choose to prepare your own mix, the following basic recipes should meet your needs. The ingredients for a homemade houseplant mix are often the same as those in commercial mixes. Purchase ingredients at reputable nurseries and garden centers.

Basic Soilless Mix

This is a general-purpose soilless mix well suited to most kinds of indoor plants.

1 quart coarse peat moss
1 quart medium-grade vermiculite
1 quart medium-grade perlite
3 tablespoons dolomite lime
1 cup sifted horticultural charcoal

Soil-based Mix

This heavier mix is especially useful for plants you don't want to repot annually.

1 part coarse sand *or*
1 part pasteurized garden loam
    (Spread loam on a cookie sheet, sprinkle water on it, and bake it in a 200° F oven for two hours. Be prepared: It smells!)
1 part basic soilless mix or commercial soilless mix

Epiphytic Mix

This mix is suitable for orchids and bromeliads, which derive much of their moisture and nutrients from the air.

1 quart long-strand sphagnum moss
1 quart coarse bark
1 quart coarse-grade perlite
1 tablespoon dolomite lime
1 cup sifted horticultural charcoal

Cactus Mix

This mix is ideal for cacti and succulents, and also for top-heavy plants, which need weighty soil.

2 quarts pasteurized *well-draining* garden loam
1 quart coarse sand
1 quart calcined clay
2 tablespoons dolomite lime
½ cup sifted horticultural charcoal

5

Plant correctly

Water the plant an hour before potting. Select a larger pot—1 to 2 inches more in diameter. For clay pots, put a piece of crockery (broken clay pot) over the bottom hole. To loosen the plant, put one hand over the soil with the stem between your fingers. Turn the pot over and rap it against a hard surface. If the soil and roots don't come out easily, run a knife between the pot and the soil to loosen them. If roots are matted, make a few shallow cuts along the outer edges of the rootball—new roots will sprout there.

Slide out soil and roots.

Support plant base.

Transfer the plant from one pot to another as quickly as possible. Partly fill the new container with the appropriate planting mix. Place the plant in the center of the pot at the height it grew in its original container. Firm the soil around the rootball, then fill the container with more soil ½ to 1 inch below the rim. Tamp it with your fingers, especially near the edges of the container. Water the plant thoroughly right away and keep the soil moist for several weeks until the plant is well established.

Loosen roots.

Insert plant in moist potting mix.

6 Repot as needed

If a plant needs daily watering, it has probably grown too many roots for its container and needs a larger one. Long root strands coming out of the drainage hole or a rootball that fills the pot completely also indicate that it's time to repot. To see whether roots are compacted and crowded, turn the plant on its side and knock the pot gently against a solid surface to loosen the rootball. If it doesn't come out, the soil may be too wet. Let it dry a little and then try again.

Massed roots

T I P : If you want to change types of potting mixes, gently wash all of the old mix off the plant's roots before repotting.

Repot plants with matted, crowded roots. Prune off roots that are circling the rootball. Use a sharp knife to make a few shallow cuts from the top of the rootball to the bottom, or loosen bound roots with your fingers. For large pots, run a blunt knife around the edge. Pull out the plant carefully—have a helper steady the pot. Repot the plant as described on pages 22 to 23. Use a new container not more than 2 to 3 inches wider at the rim than the previous one. Use the same basic type of soil mix as before.

Cut to loosen rootball.

Tap with wood block.

Support plant.

Pull pot away.

Hold plant.

Caring for Houseplants

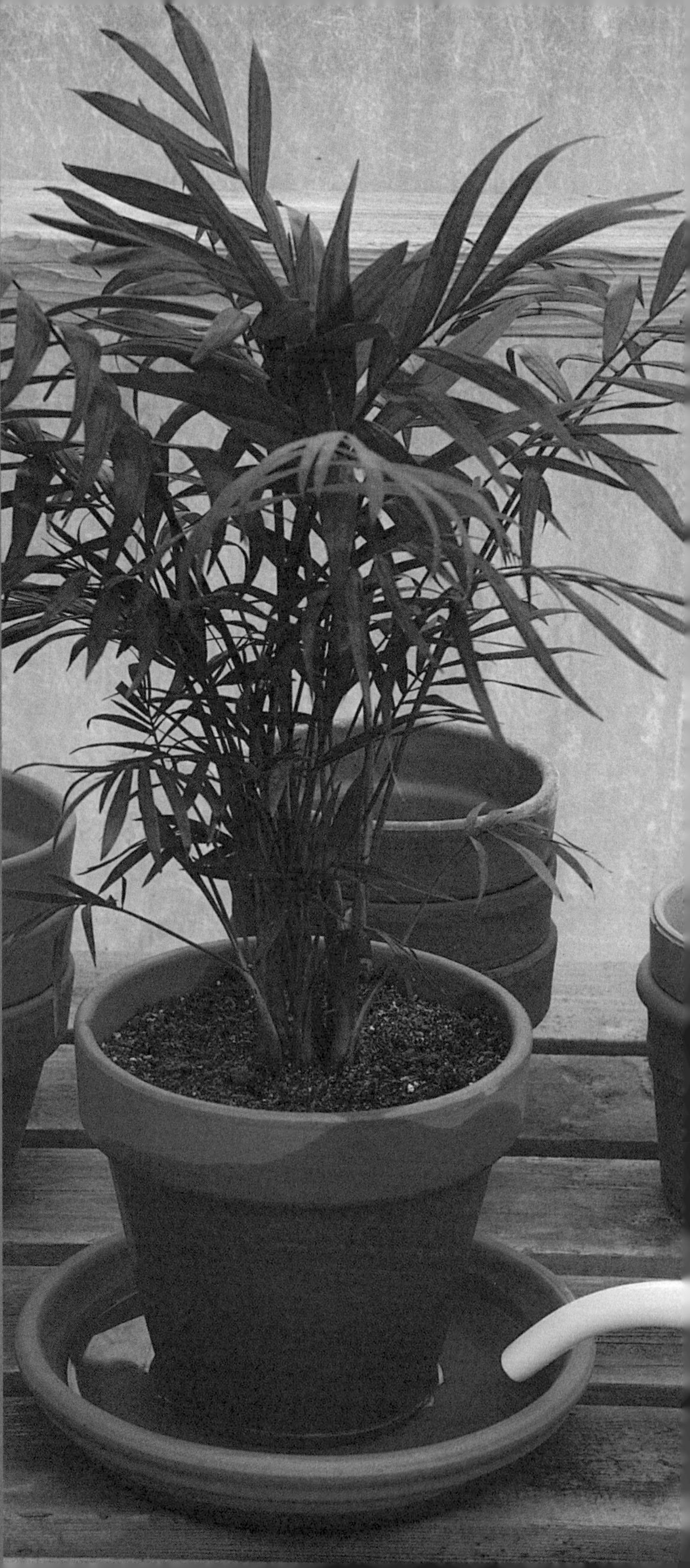

1 Use the right tools

A few simple tools will make your indoor gardening easier. Use a watering can with a long spout to water hard-to-reach plants. Sharp pruning shears or scissors ensure clean cuts. A trowel helps when transplanting. Use cloths, sponges, and a feather duster to keep leaves free of dust and grime. Light meters indicate whether the light in a particular spot is low, moderate, or high. Moisture meters indicate the level of moisture in the soil. Most of these items are available at home and garden centers and hardware stores.

2 Provide humidity

Most plants need more humidity than is usually found in a home, especially when the furnace or air conditioner is on. To increase humidity, place plants in bathrooms and kitchens or use a portable or built-in humidifier. You can also set up waterproof trays or saucers filled with pebbles or small rocks; add water to just below the surface of the pebbles and place the plants on top of them. As the water evaporates, it moistens the surrounding air. Add water as needed. Grouping plants together also helps raise humidity.

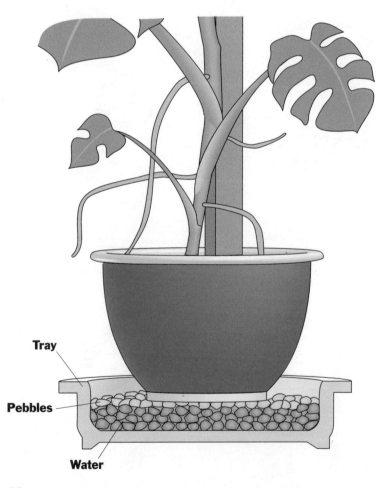

Tray

Pebbles

Water

3

Control the temperature

Most houseplants do well in average home temperatures. To encourage best growth, turn the thermostat down at night. Plants like a 10° F drop after dark, which is similar to what they experience in nature. For plants that like cool conditions, keep the thermostat between 60° and 70° F in the day and lower at night. For plants that like high temperatures, set the thermostat in the high 70s during the day and lower at night. To prevent cold drafts or blasts of hot air near plants, keep plants away from cold windows and heaters in winter.

Houseplant Temperatures

	32°F	40°F	50°F	60°F	70°F	80°F
Seeds					███████	
Cuttings					██████	
Succulents				████		
Ferns				████		
Cacti				████		
Palms*				████		
Most other houseplants*			████████			
Hardy bulbs before flowering	████████					

*Palms and most other houseplants usually grow better if temperatures are 5° to 8° F cooler during their winter rest period.

████ Best range for active growth

Water correctly

Water plants when they need it—you can kill them by both over- and underwatering. Use room temperature water. If your water is high in chlorine, let it sit uncovered overnight before using it. Do not use softened water, which has a high salt content. Instead, use bottled or rainwater, or water from an outdoor faucet. The condition of the plant usually indicates when to water. Use your finger to test the moisture level in the soil about 1 to 2 inches deep. If the soil at that level is barely moist, it is time to water.

Overwatering causes . . .

- Slow growth
- Dark blotches on leaves
- Leaves to drop off while still green
- Wilted or limp leaves
- Growth of black algae on the soil

Underwatering causes . . .

- Slow growth
- Tan or white tips and edges of leaves
- Wilting
- Buds or flowers to drop
- Older leaves to die

Add water slowly until it drains through the hole in the bottom of the pot. Empty saucers about 20 to 30 minutes after watering. If the plant is too heavy to lift, use a turkey baster to remove the water. Submerge pots to their rim about once a month by placing them in a sink or tub and leaving them there until the air bubbles have stopped. Three or four times a year, leach the potting mix by putting the plant in a sink or tub and watering it several times, letting the water drain out each time.

Watering from above

Watering from below

Water plants with fuzzy leaves from below to prevent leaves from rotting.

5 Apply fertilizer

For most indoor plants, buy a high-quality balanced dry or liquid houseplant fertilizer (such as 10-5-5), or one especially formulated for blooming plants. When applying fertilizer, always read the label and follow the directions carefully. Do not exceed the recommended amount—excess fertilizer can burn roots and leaves. Make sure the potting mix is moist before using any type of fertilizer. If using a liquid type, or powders or crystals that have to be mixed with water, apply with a watering can when watering the plant.

Fertilize to prevent . . .

- Slow growth
- Susceptibility to problems
- Older leaves becoming pale or yellow
- Older leaves dying

Excess fertilizer results in . . .

- Black or dark brown tips and edges of leaves
- Wilted or limp leaves
- White salt deposit on the soil

Apply foliar sprays with a mist sprayer outside, or in a sink or tub. Spray both sides of the foliage. This type of fertilizer is rapidly absorbed and usually acts quickly to revive a plant. Spread dry fertilizer evenly on top of the soil, lightly cultivate it in by hand, and water. Slow-release tablets, spikes, or coated pellets are convenient, as they can be inserted into the mixture and left to dispense their nutrients gradually. Plants need little fertilizer in the winter—fertilize them more in the spring and summer when they are growing more actively.

Liquid
fertilizer

Foliar
spray

Slow-
release
spike

Slow-release
tablet (use
a pencil to
insert)

33

6 Pinch and prune

Pinch back plants to keep them from getting "leggy"—with large gaps between leaves. When you pinch off a young stem tip on a soft-stemmed variety (such as coleus, begonia, or wandering-Jew), the plant will branch out below the pinch and become bushier and healthier. Use your thumb and forefinger to pinch off the growing tip as soon as the stem has four to six leaves. The buds lower down the stem, just below where you cut, will become side branches. Once they start to grow, pinch off their tips and they'll become bushy as well.

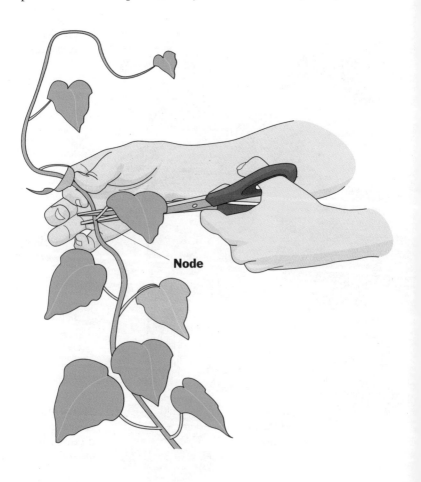

Node

Prune to remove woody stems. Before you cut, consider the effect you'd like to achieve. If you want the plant to be short and bushy, prune the top. If you want it to grow tall and thin, prune the side branches. With small, sharp pruning shears, make each cut just above a leaf. For a plant with one main trunk that has gotten too tall, with all the leaves bunched at the top, cut it back to about half its original height. New leaves will form, and the plant will become fuller and more attractive.

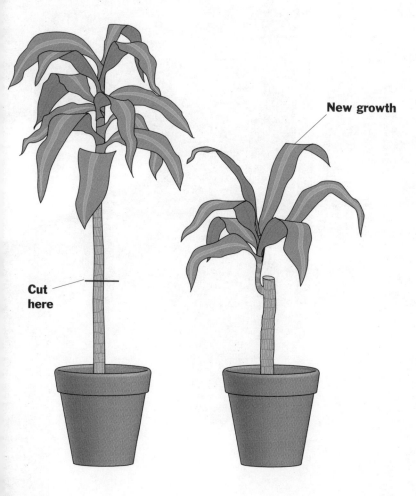

New growth

Cut here

35

1

Vacation-proof plants

A short vacation should not harm plants if they are given a thorough watering and moved away from hot, direct sun before you leave. Placing them on a tray lined with moist pebbles can also help (see page 28). For longer periods, set up a self-watering system. To keep plants healthy for two or three weeks, cover them with makeshift plastic tents. Use bamboo stakes or bent clothes hangers to support the plastic above the plant leaves. Water and mist the plant before placing it under the plastic. Set the plant in a shady spot.

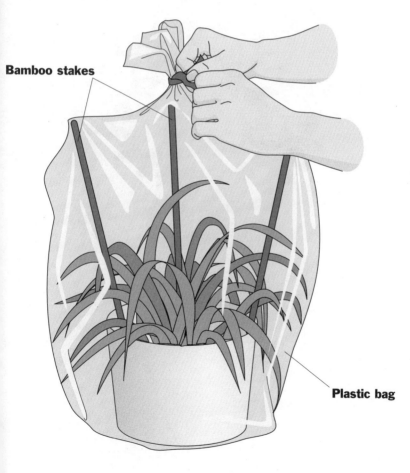

Bamboo stakes

Plastic bag

2

Care for gift plants

Remove the foil from around the pot or make
a hole in the bottom of it to allow water to drain
through. Set the plant in a well-lit but not too
bright area, out of drafts. Keep the soil moist but
not wet. If the plant favors low light, move it there gradually
(see page 17). If the plant is in bloom, remove faded blossoms to prolong its flowering. After it stops blooming, keep
it inside or transplant it in the garden in well-prepared soil.

Prolong flowering

3

With proper care, you can double the usual
life span of blooming plants in an indoor setting.
Plants that have been properly grown before
they start to flower will have enough nutrients
to carry them through the blooming period—so don't
fertilize them then. While in bloom, the plants should be
watered thoroughly and regularly. Keep them out of direct
sunlight or drafts of hot, dry air. Petals may burn, fade,
or wilt under hot, dry conditions. Trim off faded blooms to
encourage new buds to form.

Keep plants clean

Use a feather duster, or a cloth or sponge dampened with mild soapy water, to remove dust from smooth-leaved plants. Support the leaf in one hand while gently wiping away from the stem. Do not clean fragile new growth. Use a dry, soft cotton swab or a ½-inch paintbrush to clean fuzzy-leaved plants. If you have unsoftened water, you can clean many plants quickly in the sink or shower. Place each pot in a plastic bag, secured around the stem base to keep the soil in, then wash with lukewarm water at low to medium force.

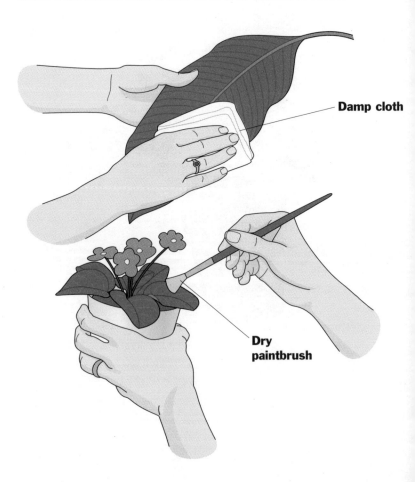

Damp cloth

Dry paintbrush

If chemical residue in the water leaves white spots, wipe them away with a soft, clean cloth. If the weather is warm, set plants outdoors in the rain, or mist large plants with a spray bottle. Remove faded flowers and leaves, and snip off brown leaf tips with sharp scissors at the same angle as the tips usually grow. Pinch off small discolored leaves at the base of their stems. Remove dead leaves that have fallen onto the top of the soil.

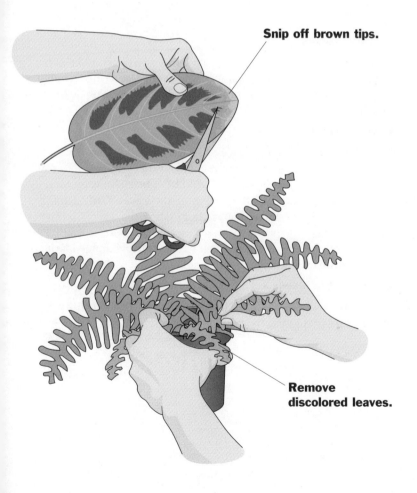

Snip off brown tips.

Remove discolored leaves.

Solve cultural problems

Each time you water, inspect plants for any problems. If one starts looking poorly, you need to become a detective to determine the cause. If the problem does not appear to be pests (see pages 44 and 45) or disease (see pages 46 and 47), look at the plant's environment and living conditions. Review your watering, fertilizing, and pruning habits against the plant's needs and compare them with the symptoms of common cultural problems (see below).

Yellowing leaves

Often caused by too little or too much light or fertilizer, too much water, or high evening temperatures. Watch your watering techniques carefully, and check if the plant needs fertilizing, especially with nitrogen and iron.

Browning leaves

When the edges and tips of leaves turn tan or light brown, it's usually because the plant hasn't been given enough water. Too much sun or high temperatures, dry air, or overfertilization may also cause this. Overwatering may cause dark blotches on the leaves. Darkened leaf edges are often the result of damage from salt in the water. To leach out the salt, flush the plant with water two or three times, waiting between each flushing until the plant has completely drained. Trim off the damaged sections, following the natural shape of the leaf.

Dry and brittle leaves

This is usually the result of too little water, or air that is too dry. Water carefully and try to raise the humidity level around the plant.

Some plants suffer from a lack of light. In this case, new growth is weak and spindly with large gaps between the leaves. Flowering plants fail to produce flowers, and plants with colorful foliage become pale. If most of the available light is coming from one source, plants bend their stems and leaves in that direction. Solve light-related problems by gradually moving afflicted plants to a brighter location. Be sure to keep plants that are in direct sun well watered.

Spotted leaves

White to light yellow blotches in various patterns on older leaves, especially fuzzy ones, are usually caused when cool water is splashed on them during watering. Avoid this when applying water, or use tepid water, which won't cause as much spotting.

Wilting

Too much sun or high temperatures or too much or too little water cause this problem. Move the wilted plant to another location and water deeply when the potting mix starts to dry out.

Spindly growth

This occurs when the plant is not receiving enough light. Pinch back or prune the excess growth and gradually move the plant to a brighter location.

Lack of blooms

High evening temperatures and lack of light sometimes cause this. A cooler, well-lit spot is one solution, or move the plant to a cooler location at night.

Control pests

The best control for pests is prevention. When you bring home a new plant, keep it isolated for the first week if possible and watch closely for insects. If at any time you put your plants outside, check them carefully when you bring them back in. Keep plants clean and free of dust and remove dead leaves from the plant and the soil surface (see pages 40 and 41).

Common Pests

Aphids   Tiny wingless, green, soft-bodied insects causing new leaves to be curled, discolored, and smaller than normal. They excrete a honeydew, which is sticky to the touch. Wipe off small infestations, or use a houseplant insect spray.

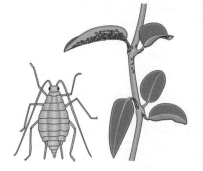

Mealybugs   These white cottony or waxy insects up to ¼ inch long cluster on the undersides of leaves, on stems, and in the crotches where leaves are attached. Honeydew may cover the leaves. Dab each bug with a cotton swab dipped in rubbing alcohol and then rinse leaves with clear water; or use a houseplant insect spray—several applications may be necessary.

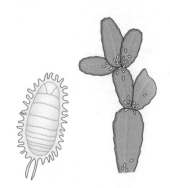

If insects appear, isolate the infected plant and wash or scrape off bugs or dab them with a cotton swab dipped in rubbing alcohol. If that doesn't work, use a pesticide or insecticidal soap—read the label carefully and follow all directions. Take the plant outside to spray it. Ferns and other sensitive plants are especially endangered by many types of chemicals, so be careful. If there is no way to cure a plant, discard it and its soil and then wash the container thoroughly.

Common Pests (continued)

Scale   Looking like white, cottony clumps—or brown or reddish hard-shelled bumps—scale line up along the main veins of the plant and cause it to lose color, turn yellow, and die. Honeydew may be present. Gently scrape off scale with a fingernail or soft toothbrush, wash the plant with lukewarm soapy water (use a mild liquid detergent), or use a houseplant insect spray. Ferns, palms, and rubber plants are prime targets for scale.

Spider mites   Thriving in warm, dry conditions, these tiny bugs feed on the undersides of leaves. They spin fine webs along the veins and leaves, which appear stippled, yellow, and dirty. Over several weeks, use a houseplant insect spray to kill the mites as they hatch.

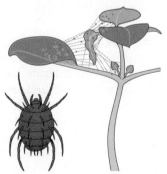

Combat diseases

Most houseplant diseases are the result of
overwatering or of moisture remaining in leaf
axils. It is under these conditions that fungi
and bacteria can thrive. Damaged leaves and
bruised stems may also provide entry for bacteria and thus
disease. Overcrowding limits air circulation and that too
can cause trouble.

Common Diseases

Crown and root rot   Usually the result
of overwatering or lack of proper drainage in the container, it causes plants to
turn brown or wilt quickly. The base of
the plant's stem becomes soft and discolored, and the roots may be dead and rot-
ted. If the plant is only mildly affected,
let the soil dry out between waterings,
or transplant into fast-draining soil. Discard badly infected plants and their soil
and completely clean the containers.

Botrytis or gray mold   Light
brown patches appear on leaves,
stems, or flowers, gradually dark-
ening and turning soft and moist.
A grayish mold covers the affected
surfaces. Infected plant parts curl
up and fall off. Remove these and
treat the rest of the plant with a
houseplant fungicide that lists that
type of plant. Avoid overly humid
air and improve air circulation around the plant. Do not mist suscepti-
ble plants.

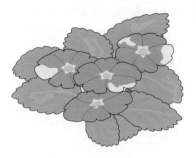

Always remove diseased sections as soon as you see them, and isolate an affected plant while you are treating it. To prevent disease, avoid splashing water on foliage and flowers, and avoid growing plants under crowded conditions where air is damp and still. Provide air circulation around plants, but protect them from drafts. Plants with persistent problems may need to be moved to warmer locations.

Common Diseases (continued)

Leaf spot   Round reddish-brown spots surrounded by a yellow margin appear on leaves. Several spots may join to form blotches. Badly spotted leaves may turn yellow and die. Clip these off and water carefully to avoid getting the foliage wet.

Powdery mildew   Powdery white or gray patches appear on leaves, stems, and flowers, beginning on the upper surface of older leaves. Tissue underneath may turn yellow or brown, and affected leaves may drop. Remove infected leaves and move the plant to where it receives more light, even air temperature, and good air circulation.

Starting New Plants

Divide plants

Plants that send up stems from a central point can be divided. Take the entire plant out of its pot and firmly but gently pull apart obviously separate sections. Each section must include a healthy root system. Wash away or remove with your hands some of the potting mixture so you can see the separate sections. If they are joined with tough roots, use a sharp knife to cut through the rootball. Place the divided sections into their own containers, fill with potting mix, and water. Set them in indirect light for a week or two to adjust.

Plant seeds

Houseplant seeds are available from some garden centers and a few mail-order nurseries. Use flats, cartons, pots, or small plastic trays with clear covers for planting. Use a fine, sterile growing medium such as potting soil, sand, or an equal mixture of vermiculite, perlite, and peat moss. Scatter tiny dustlike seeds on top of the moist medium and leave them uncovered. Sow medium-sized seeds and cover with a thin layer of the mix. Cover large seeds to a depth twice their diameter. Label each seed type with its name and the date it was planted.

Houseplants to Grow From Seed

Botanical Name	Common Name
Agapanthus	Agapanthus, blue African lily, lily-of-the-Nile
Aglaonema modestum	Chinese evergreen
Asparagus	Asparagus fern
Begonia × semperflorens-cultorum	Wax begonia
Bromeliaceae	Bromeliads
Browallia	Browallia, sapphire-flower
Cactaceae	Cacti
Campanula	Star-of-Bethlehem, bellflower
Carissa macrocarpa	Ornamental pepper
Citrus species	Citrus
Coffea arabica	Coffee plant
Coleus × hybridus	Coleus
Crossandra infundibuliformis	Crossandra, firecracker-flower
Cuphea ignea	Cigar plant
Cyclamen persicum	Cyclamen
Exacum affine	Persian violet
Felicia amelloides	Blue marguerite, blue daisy
Gesneriaceae	Gesneriads
Hypoestes phyllostachya	Hypoestes, pink-polka-dot, freckle-face
Impatiens species	Impatiens
Palmae	Palms
Pelargonium	Florist's geraniums
Peperomia species	Peperomia
Persea americana	Avocado
Primula	Primrose
Thunbergia alata	Black-eyed-susan, thunbergia

Cover the container with glass or plastic, place on a heating pad or on top of the refrigerator, following lighting recommendations on the seed packet. Mist the medium when it starts to dry. When the seedlings emerge, remove the cover and put the container in brighter light. Transplant when seedlings have at least two sets of leaves. Dig them out carefully and place them into individual pots filled with potting mix. Water again and move plants progressively to brighter light. Fertilize at half the suggested rate twice a month for two to three months.

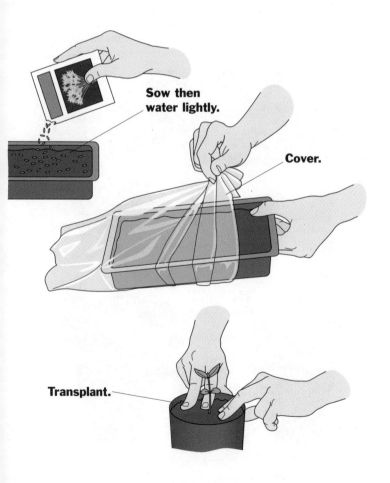

Sow then water lightly.

Cover.

Transplant.

3 Take stem cuttings

Most plants with soft stems can be propagated using stem cuttings. Take cuttings 3 to 4 inches long with at least four healthy leaves. Cut with a sharp pair of hand shears or scissors just below the node—where a leaf grows from the stem. Pull off the lowest one or two leaves on the cutting, dip the end in rooting hormone (available at nurseries), and place in plastic pots or a seed flat filled with moist rooting medium made of 1 part sand and 1 part peat moss, or 2 parts perlite and 1 part peat moss.

Geranium **Coleus**

Carnation **Fibrous begonia**

Make a hole in the rooting medium with a pencil. Insert the stem portion of the cutting and firm the mix around it. Encase the container in a clear plastic bag. Use a stake or loop of wire to support the plastic so it does not touch the leaves. Punch a few ventilation holes in the top (or open the bag every day or two). Set the container in a bright, warm place out of direct sunlight. After two weeks, gently tug on a growing cutting. If its roots are ½ to 1 inch long, it is ready for transplanting.

Impatiens **Succulents**

Ficus **Chrysanthemum**

4 Use leaf cuttings

Cut a mature leaf from the parent plant. Cut the leaf stem ½ to 1 inch long. Set the leaf in moistened rooting medium at a 45-degree angle (it can be resting against the side of the container). Do not place the cut end too deep in the mix. Cover with a clear plastic bag or cup to create a greenhouse effect. In a few weeks, you will see tiny plants growing at the base of the leaf. When the new plants have leaves the size of a nickel, lift them out, cut away the parent leaf, and transplant.

Root plantlets

Some plants reproduce by sending out miniature plants on runners, or shoots. When these plantlets begin to form aerial roots, they can be separated from the parent. Root them by filling a small pot with moist rooting medium and placing it alongside the parent plant. Without severing the runner, lay the plantlet on top of the rooting mix in the new pot and hold it in place with a hairpin. Keep the rooting mix moist. When the plantlet begins to grow, the stem between it and the parent plant can be cut and discarded.

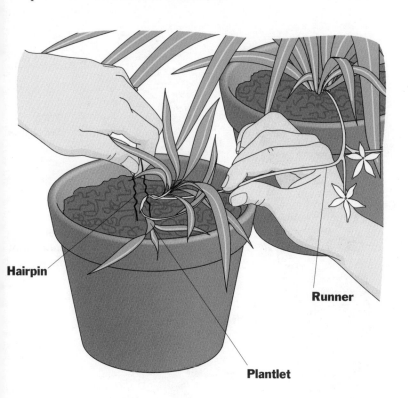

Hairpin

Runner

Plantlet

6 Air-layer certain types

Air-layer schefflera, dieffenbachia, ficus, and dracaena species that have lost their bottom leaves.
Using a sharp knife, cut into, but not through,
the side stem or main trunk about one-third of
the way down. Insert a wedge such as a matchstick to keep
the cut open. Wrap the stem with a large handful of wet
sphagnum moss, cover with plastic wrap, and secure with
string or wire twist ties above and below the cut. When
new roots form in the moss, cut off the stem just below the
rooted section, remove the plastic, and pot the new plant.

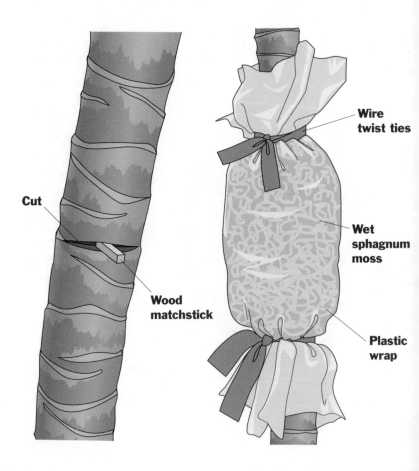

Cut

Wood
matchstick

Wire
twist ties

Wet
sphagnum
moss

Plastic
wrap

7

Divide tubers, bulbs, and corms

Tuber division works for large bulbs of florist's gloxinia, tuberous begonia, and caladium. Simply cut the tuber with a knife as you would a seed potato, making sure that every part has a bud, or "eye." Dust the cut surface with fungicide, let it dry, and plant each piece just below the surface of a moist rooting medium. The glory lily produces cigar-shaped tubers—break them into pieces and replant. For plants with corms, such as freesias, separate and replant (about 2 inches deep) many of the small new corms that form around the parent corm.

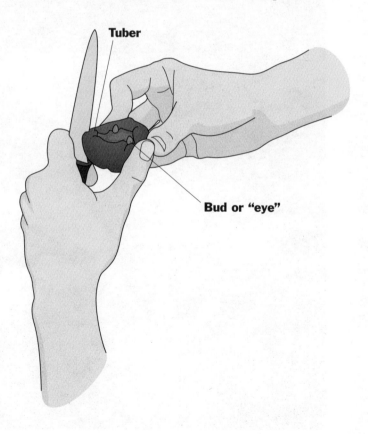

Tuber

Bud or "eye"

Houseplants for Special Purposes

The lists in this section recommend a wide variety of houseplants for their size, colorful flowers and leaves, and special cultural needs. Decide the qualities you want in a houseplant—size, easiness, flower or leaf color, or a plant to fit in a "difficult" spot—then select plants from these lists to get just the right plant for your home.

Cast-iron plant

Dumb-cane

EASY-TO-GROW TYPES

Aglaonema   Chinese evergreen

Aspidistra   Cast-iron plant

Chlorophytum   Spider plant

Dieffenbachia   Dumb-cane

Dracaenas   Corn plant

Monstera deliciosa   Split-leaf philodendron

Philodendron scandens ssp. *oxycardium*   Heartleaf philodendron

Plectranthus australis   Swedish ivy, creeping-charlie

Sansevieria trifasciata 'Laurentii' Snake plant

Spathiphyllum   White anthurium, peace lily

PLANTS THAT NEED HIGH HUMIDITY

Adiantum   Maidenhair fern

Asplenium nidus   Bird's-nest fern

Davallia   Rabbitfoot fern

Fittonia   Nerve plant

Gynura aurantiaca   Velvet plant

Maranta leuconeura   Prayer plant

Nephrolepis exaltata 'Bostoniensis' Boston fern

Pandanus veitchii   Screw pine

Pileas   Aluminum plant, artillery plant

Polyscias fruticosa   Ming aralia

Pteris ferns   Table, fan-table, brake, ribbon, and silverleaf fern

Saintpaulia   African violet

Schefflera   Umbrella tree

Schefflera elegantissima   False-aralia

Rubber plant

Croton

PLANTS THAT TOLERATE LOW HUMIDITY

Aglaonema Chinese evergreen

Ceropegia linearis ssp. *woodii* Rosaryvine, string-of-hearts

Chlorophytum Spider plant

Chrysalidocarpus lutescens Butterfly palm

Dracaena Corn plant

Ficuses Weeping Chinese fig, rubber plant

Hedera helix English ivy

Nolina recurvata Ponytail palm, bottle palm

Plectranthus australis Swedish ivy, creeping-charlie

Sansevieria trifasciata 'Laurentii' Snake plant

Tradescantia Various variegated varieties of wandering-Jew

PLANTS WITH COLORFUL LEAVES

Aglaonema Chinese evergreen

Codiaeum japonica Croton

Dieffenbachia Dumb-cane

Dracaenas Variegated varieties of corn plant

Epipremnum aureum Pothos, devil's-ivy

Fittonia Nerve plant

Gynura aurantiaca Velvet plant

Iresine Bloodleaf

Maranta leuconeura Prayer plant

Plectranthus oertendahlii Royal-charlie, prostrate coleus

Tradescantia Various variegated varieties of wandering-Jew

Cyclamen

Bird's-nest fern

FLOWERING PLANTS

Anthurium   Flamingoflower

Aphelandra squarrosa   Aphelandra, zebra plant

Bromeliads

Calceolaria crenatiflora   Calceolaria pocketbook plant

Chlorophytum   Spider plant

Cyclamen persicum   Cyclamen

Kalanchoe blossfeldiana   Flaming-katy

Saintpaulia   African violet

Schlumbergera   Christmas cactus

Spathiphyllum   White anthurium, peace lily

SMALL PLANTS
(less than 1 foot tall or long)

Adiantum   Maidenhair fern

Asplenium nidus   Bird's-nest fern

Dracaena surculosa   Golddust dracaena

Fittonia   Nerve plant

Iresine   Bloodleaf

Kalanchoes

Peperomias

Pileas   Aluminum plant, artillery plant

Saintpaulia   African violet

Tolmiea menziesii   Piggyback plant

Spider plant

Swedish ivy

MEDIUM-SIZED PLANTS
(between 1 and 3 feet tall)

Aglaonema   Chinese evergreen

Asparagus densiflorus 'Sprengeri'
Asparagus fern

Aspidistra   Cast-iron plant

Bromeliads

Ceropegia linearis ssp. *woodii*
Rosary vine (string of hearts)

Chlorophytum   Spider plant

Cissus antarctica   Kangaroo vine

Cissus rhombifolia   Grape ivy

Cyrtomium falcatum   Holly fern

Dracaena deremensis   Dragon
tree, ribbon plant

Epipremnum aureum   Pothos,
devil's-ivy

Gynura aurantiaca   Velvet plant

Hedera helix   English ivy

Maranta leuconeura   Prayer plant

Nephrolepis exaltata 'Bostoniensis'
Boston fern

Pandanus veitchii   Screw pine

Plectranthus   Swedish ivy,
creeping-charlie

Phlebodium aureum   Bear's-paw
fern, hare's-foot fern

Pteris ferns   Table, fan-table,
brake, ribbon, and silverleaf
fern

Sansevieria trifasciata 'Laurentii'
Snake plant

Sedum morganianum   Donkey's-
tail, burro's-tail

Spathiphyllum   White anthurium,
peace lily

Syngonium   Arrowhead vine

Tradescantia   Wandering-Jew

Split-leaf philodendron

String-of-beads

LARGE/TALL PLANTS
(3 feet tall or long)

Araucaria columnaris   Norfolk Island pine

Chamaedorea elegans   Parlor palm

Chrysalidocarpus lutescens   Butterfly palm

Dieffenbachia   Dumb-cane

Dracaenas   Corn plant

Fatsia japonica   Japanese aralia

Ficus benjamina   Weeping fig

Ficus elastica   Rubber plant

Ficus lyrata   Fiddleleaf fig

Howea forsteriana   Kentia palm

Monstera deliciosa   Split-leaf philodendron

Nolina recurvata   Ponytail palm, bottle palm

Philodendron bipinnatifidum   Lacey-tree philodendron

Philodendron domesticum   Spade-leaf philodendron

Philodendron scandens ssp. *oxycardium*   Heartleaf philodendron

Polyscias fruticosa   Ming aralia

Schefflera   Umbrella tree

Schefflera elegantissima   False-aralia

SUCCULENTS

Succulents are easy to care for and make nice houseplants for beginning gardeners. They need a porous, fast-draining potting mix, good air circulation, and lots of light. Put them in a sunny windowsill or greenhouse window. Put them in a cool, dry place for the winter, watering only a couple of times, and most will bloom in the spring when you being watering again.

Agave   Agave, century plant

Aloe   Aloe, torch-plant, aloe vera

Crassula   Jade plant

Echeveria   Hen and chicks

Euphorbia   Crown-of-thorns, corkscrew

Kalanchoe   Felt-plant, pandaplant

Sansevieria   Snake plant

Sedum   Donkey's tail, jellybeans

Senecio   String-of-beads, rosary-plant

U.S./Metric Measure Conversions

	Symbol	Formulas for Exact Measures		To find:	Rounded Measures for Quick Reference	
		When you know:	Multiply by:			
Mass (Weight)	oz	ounces	28.35	grams	1 oz	= 30 g
	lb	pounds	0.45	kilograms	4 oz	= 115 g
	g	grams	0.035	ounces	8 oz	= 225 g
	kg	kilograms	2.2	pounds	16 oz = 1 lb	= 450 g
					32 oz = 2 lb	= 900 g
					36 oz = $2^1/_4$ lb	= 1000 g (1 kg)
Volume	pt	pints	0.47	liters	1 c	= 250 ml
	qt	quarts	0.95	liters	2 c (1pt)	= 500 ml
	gal	gallons	3.785	liters	4 c (1 qt)	= 1 liter
	ml	milliliters	0.034	fluid ounces	4 qt (1 gal)	= $3^3/_4$ liter
Length	in	inches	2.54	centimeters	$3/_8$ in	= 1.0 cm
	ft	feet	30.48	centimeters	1 in	= 2.5 cm
	yd	yards	0.9144	meters	2 in	= 5.0 cm
	mi	miles	1.609	kilometers	$2^1/_2$ in	= 6.5 cm
	km	kilometers	0.621	miles	12 in (1 ft)	= 30.0 cm
	m	meters	1.094	yards	1 yd	= 90.0 cm
	cm	centimeters	0.39	inches	100 ft	= 30.0 m
					1 mi	= 1.6 km
Temperature	°F	Fahrenheit	$5/_9$ (after subtracting 32)	Celsius	32° F	= 0° C
	°C	Celsius	$9/_5$ (then add 32)	Fahrenheit	212° F	= 100° C
Area	in^2	square inches	6.452	square centimeters	$1 in^2$	= 6.5 cm^2
	ft^2	square feet	929.0	square centimeters	$1 ft^2$	= 930 cm^2
	yd^2	square yards	8361.0	square centimeters	$1 yd^2$	= 8360 cm^2